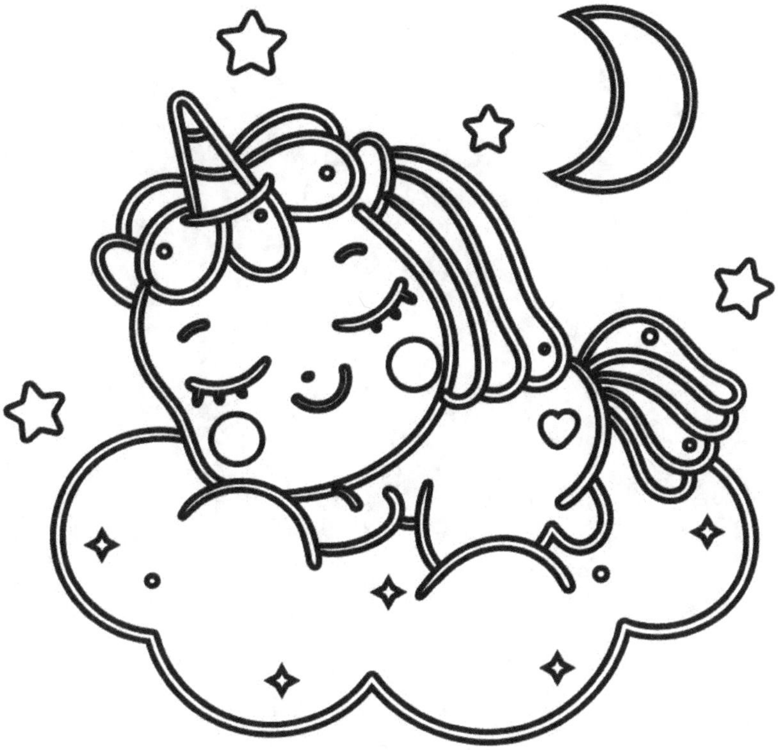

This book is for

____

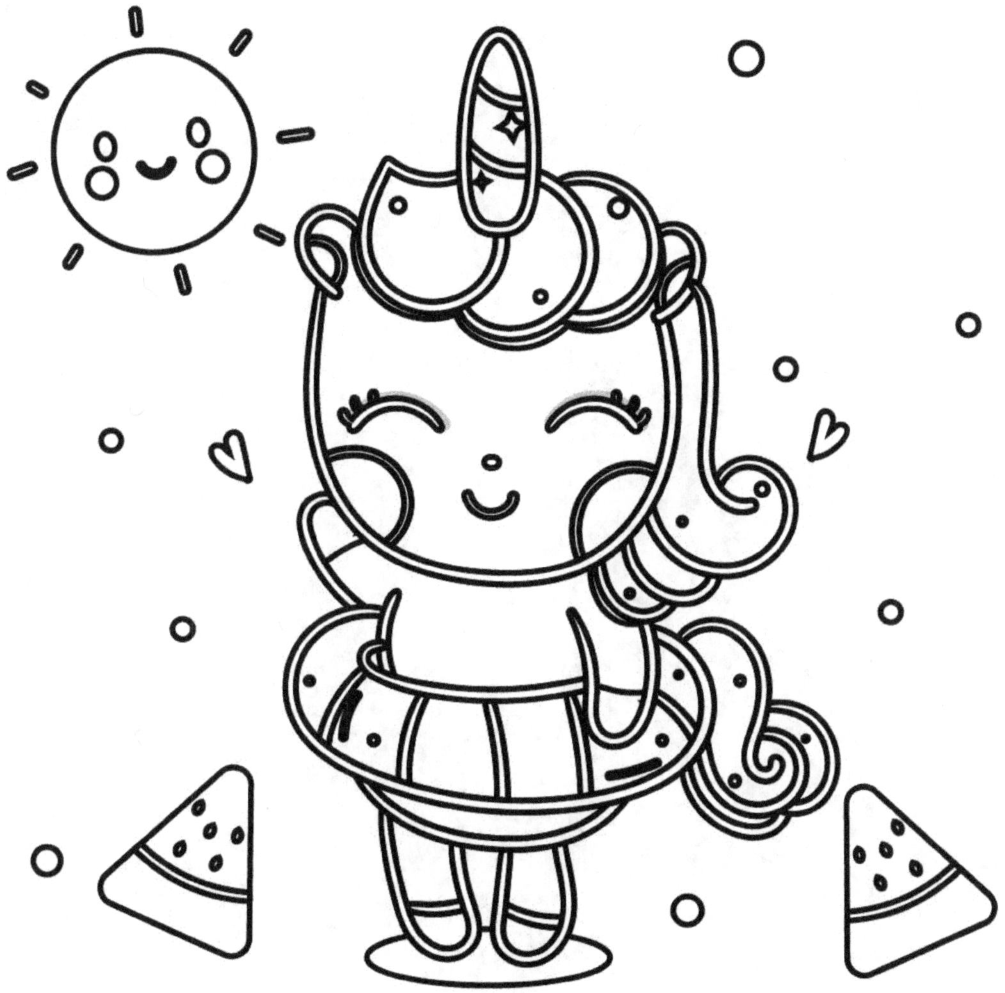

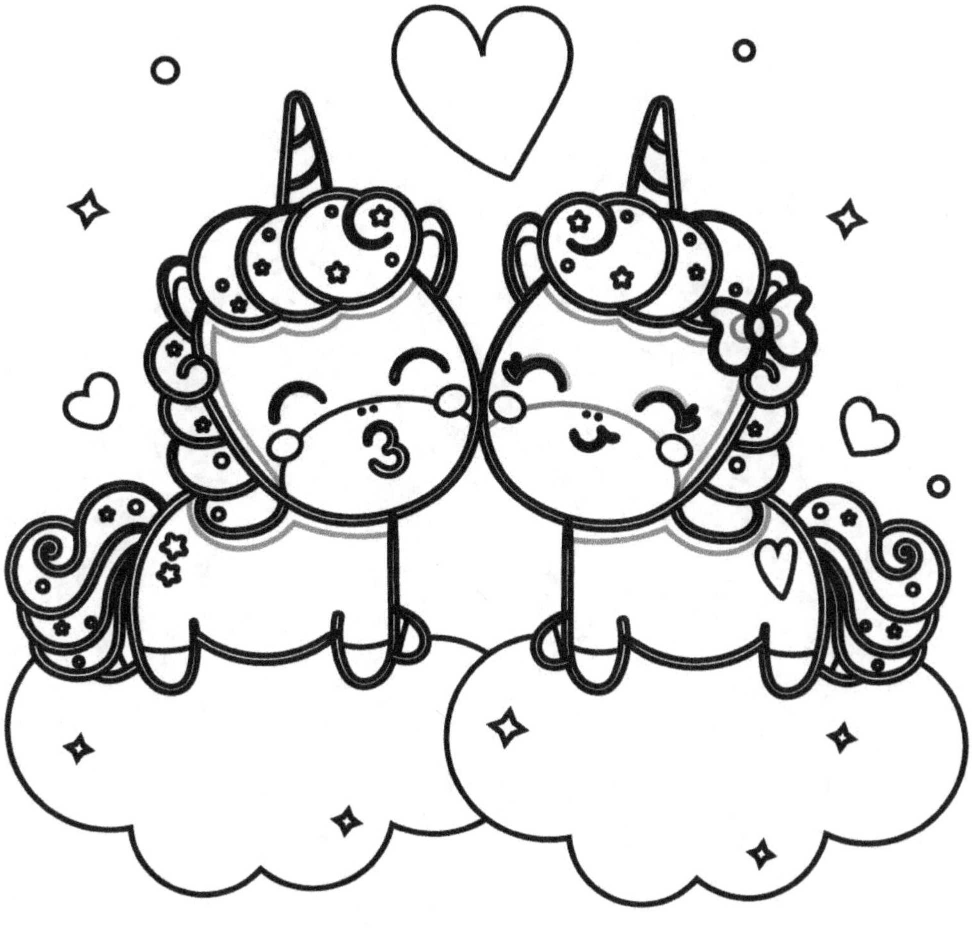

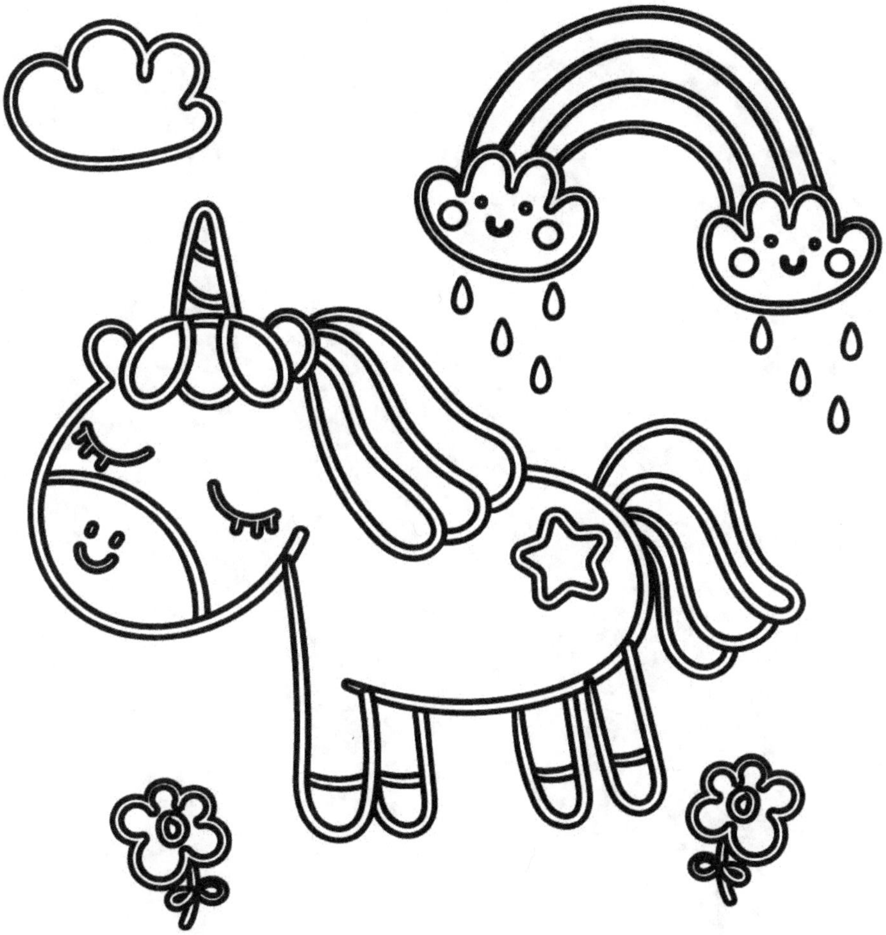

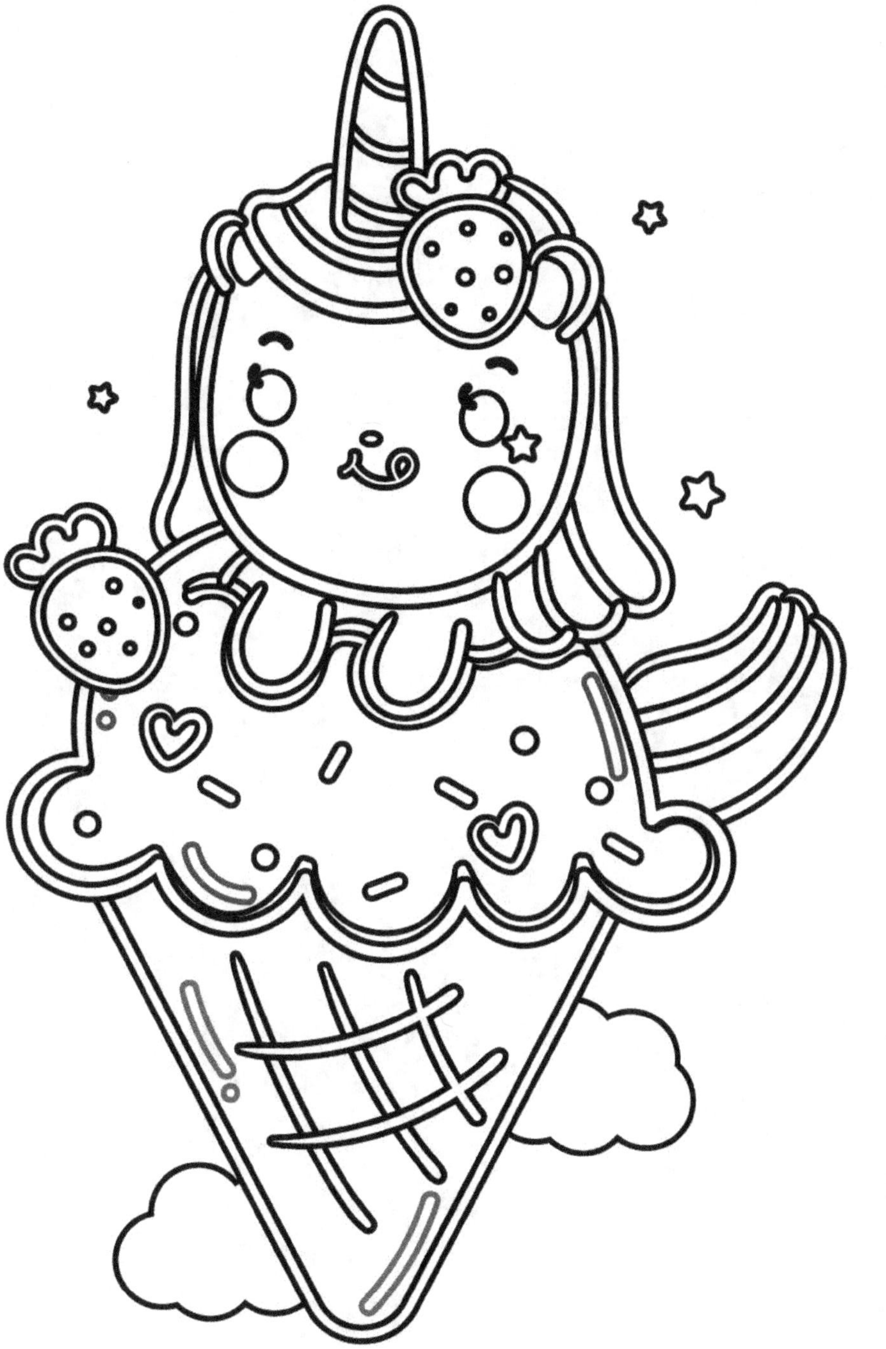

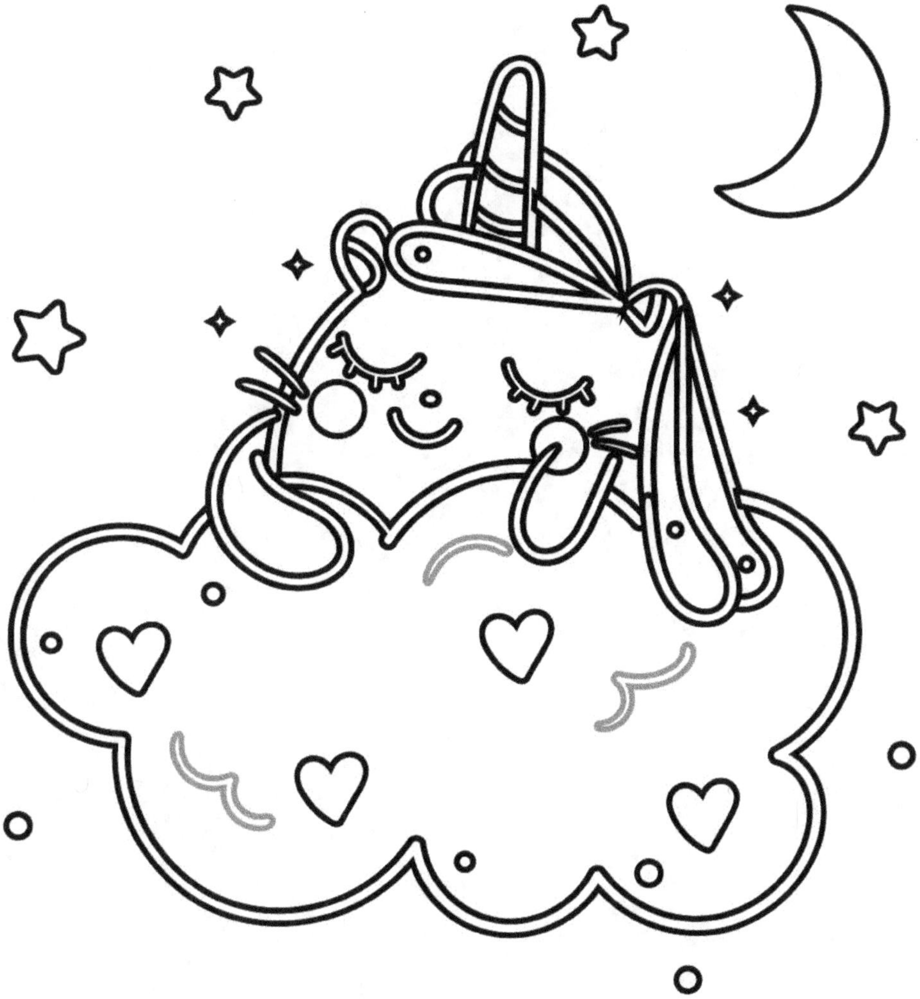

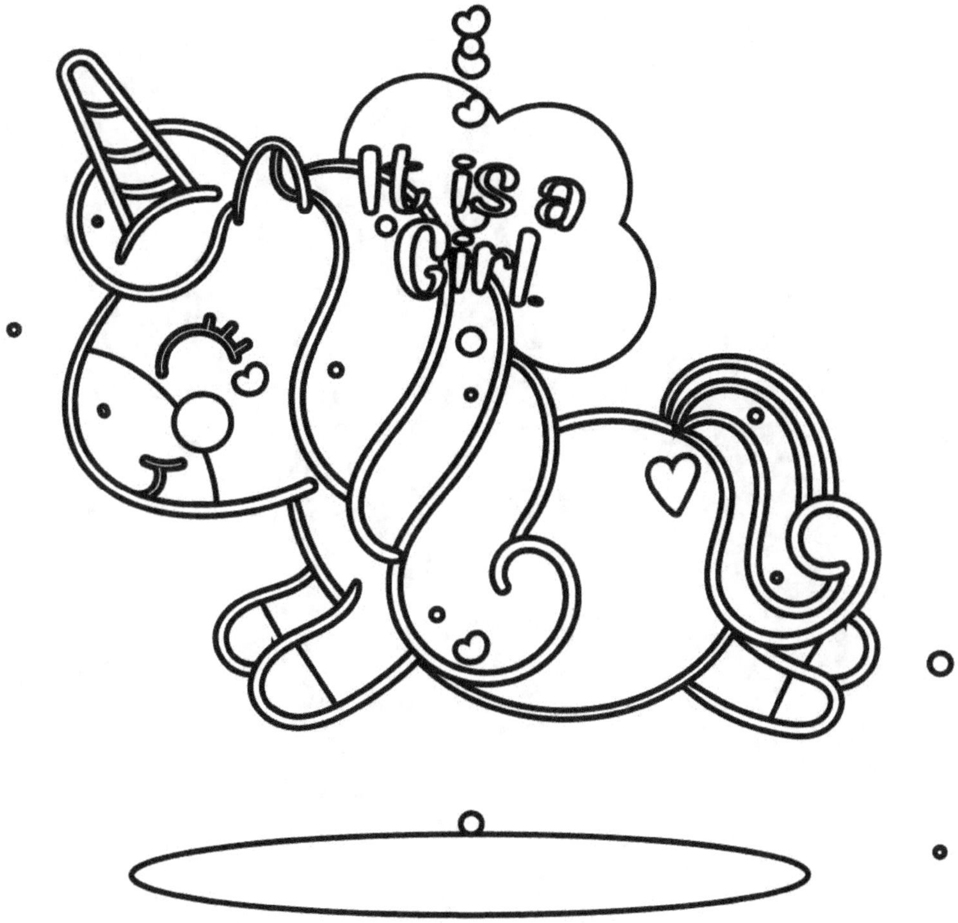
It is a
Girl

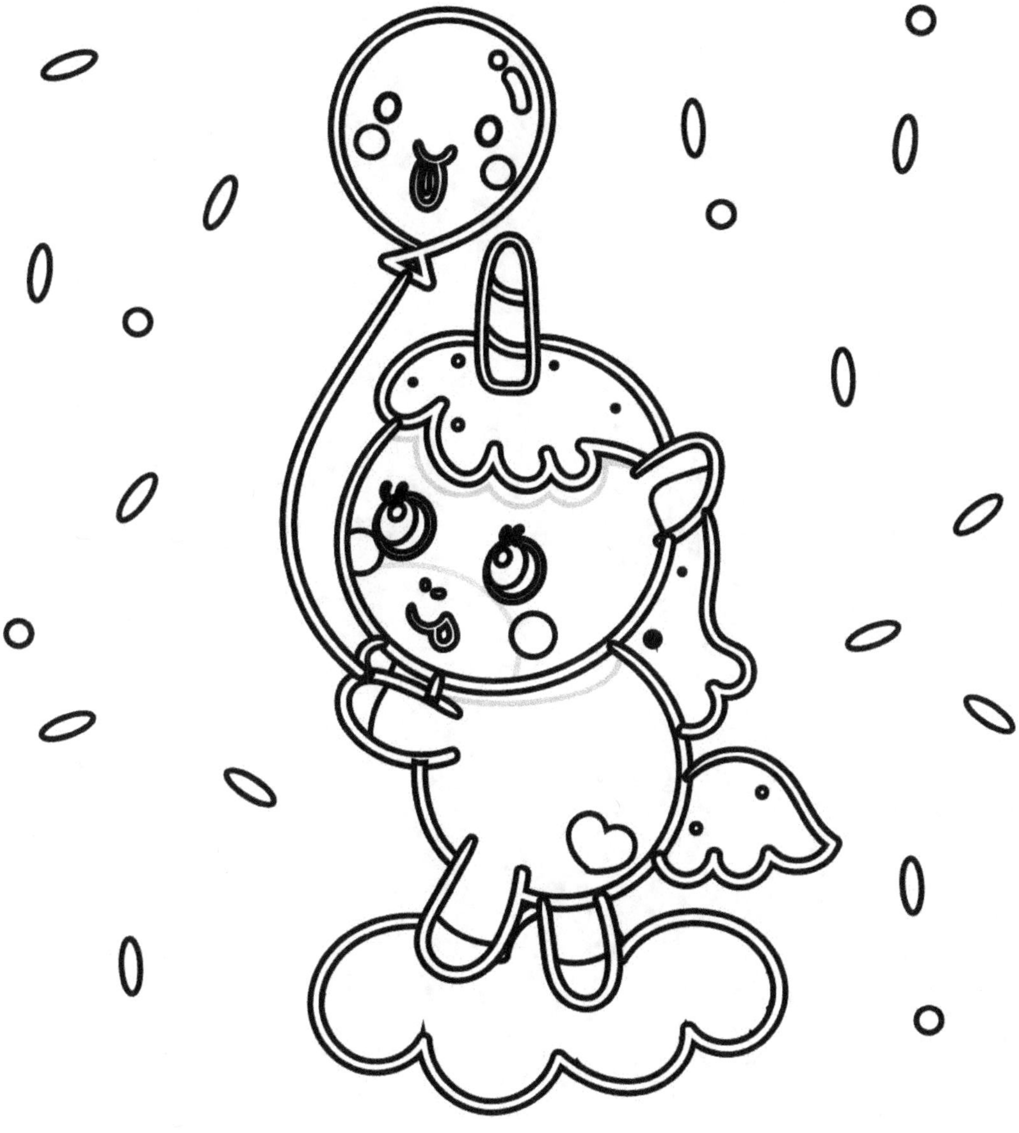

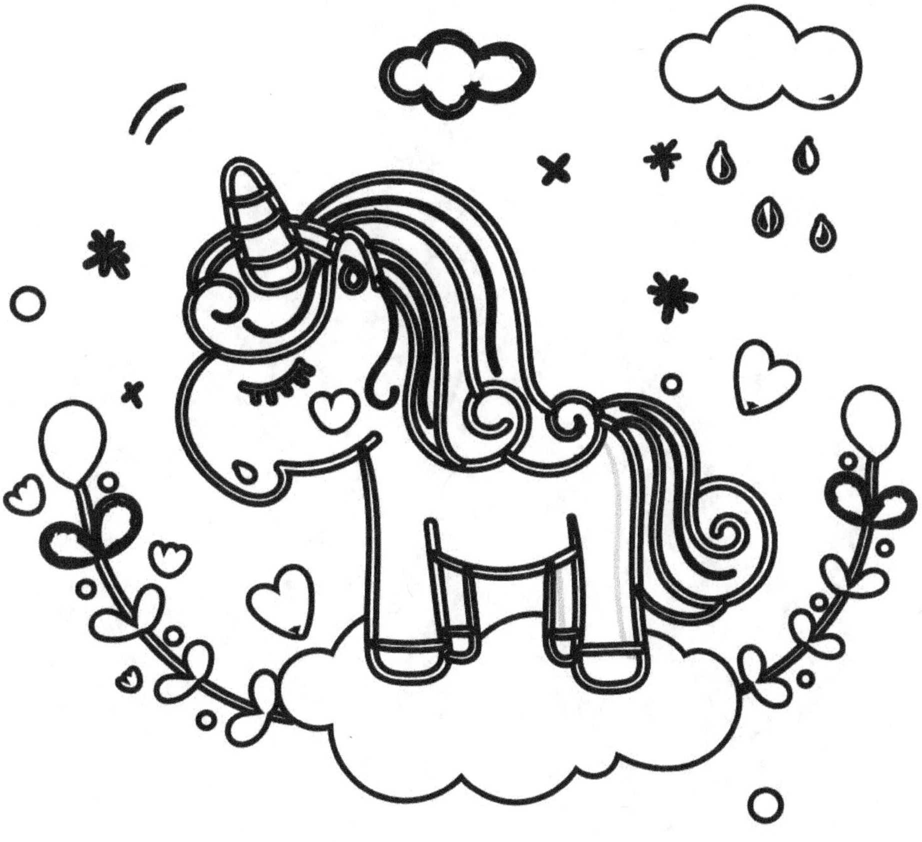

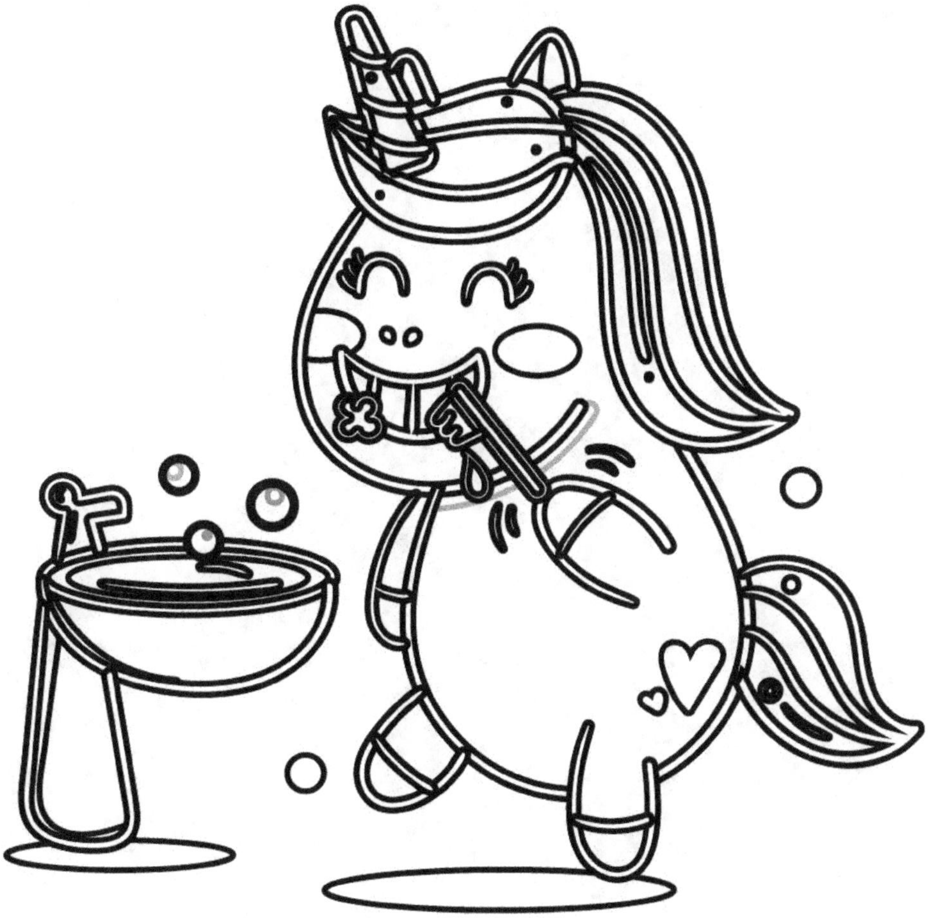

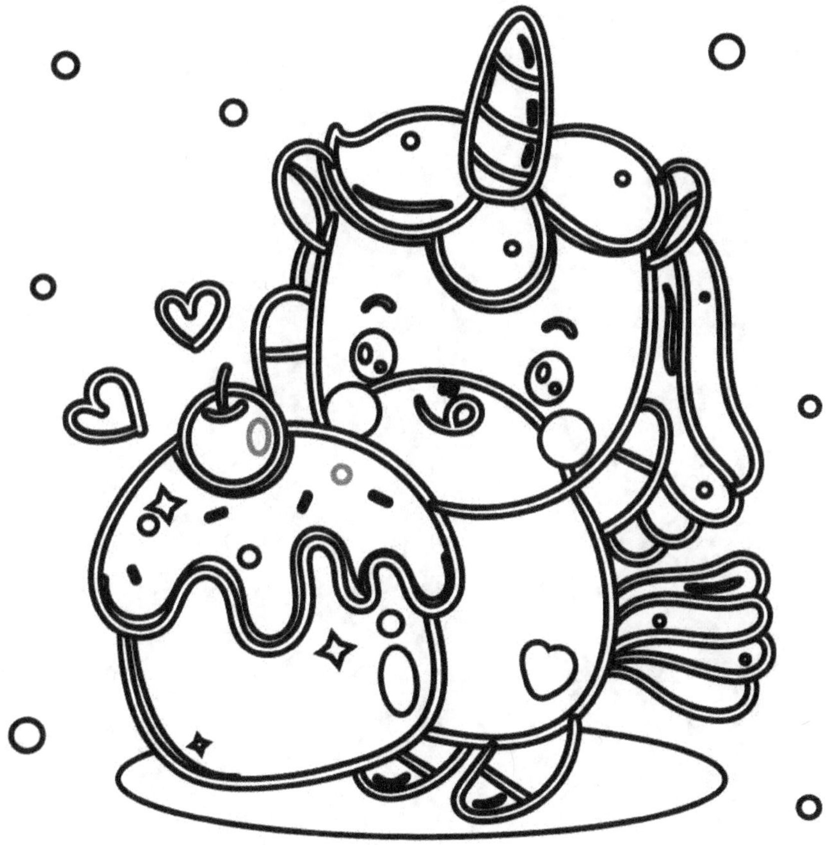

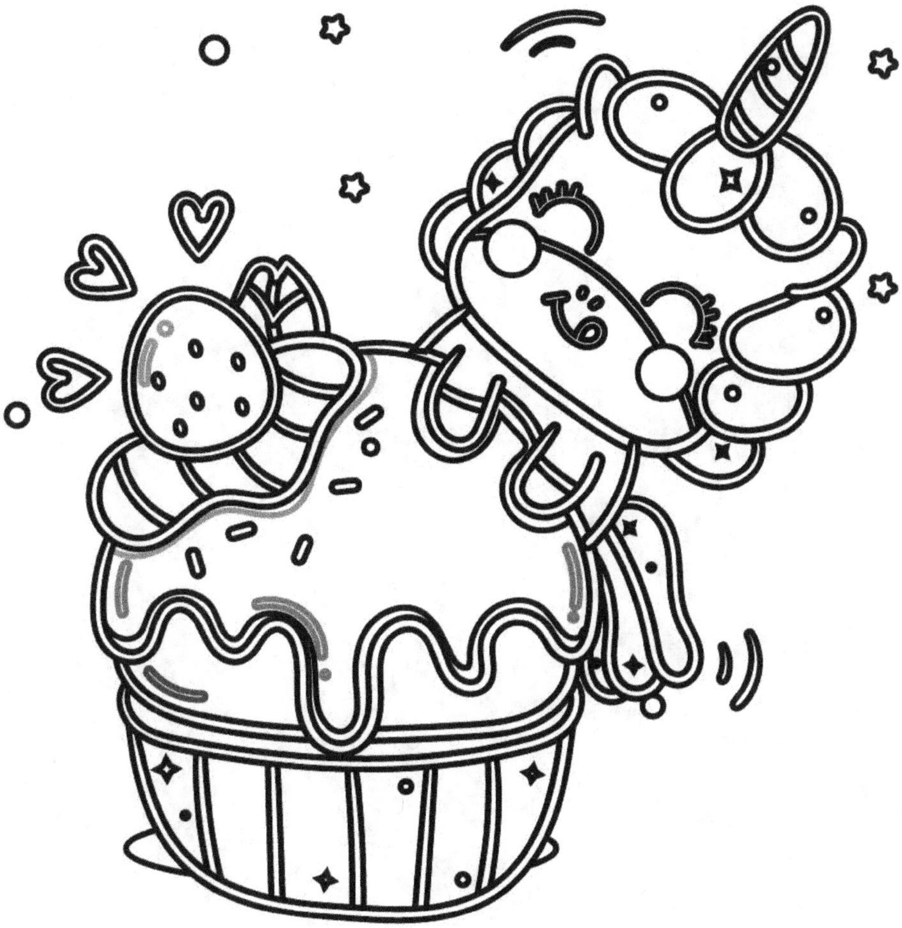

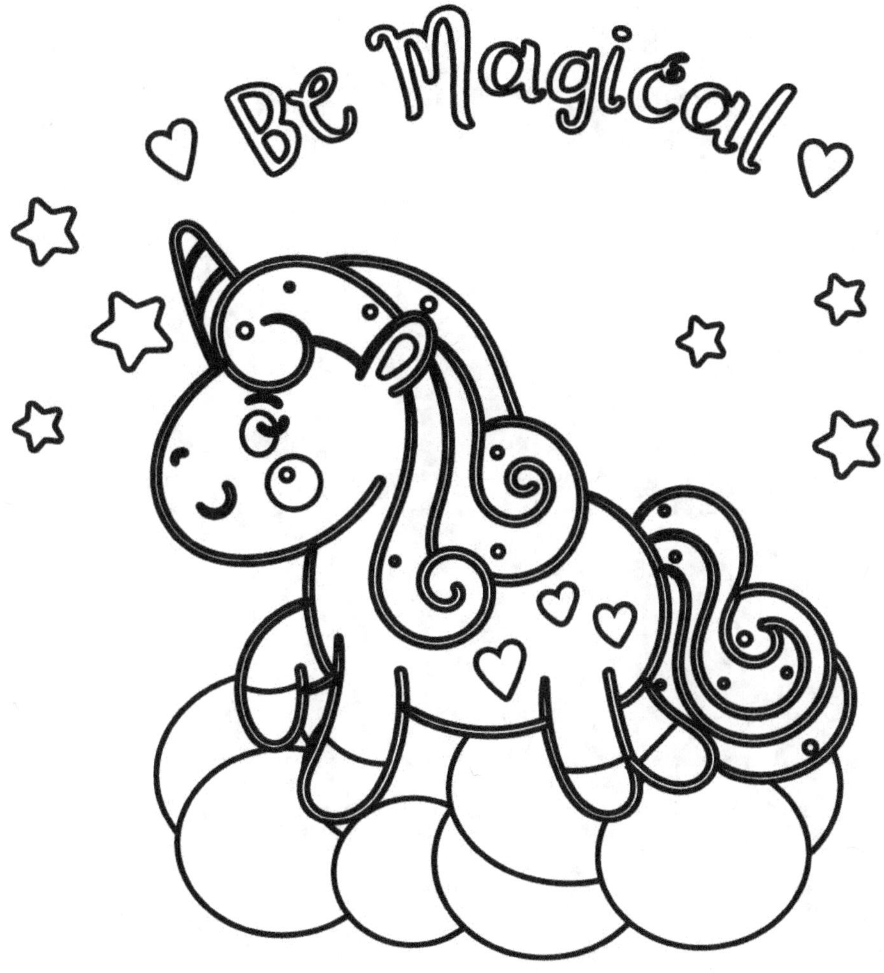
Be Magical

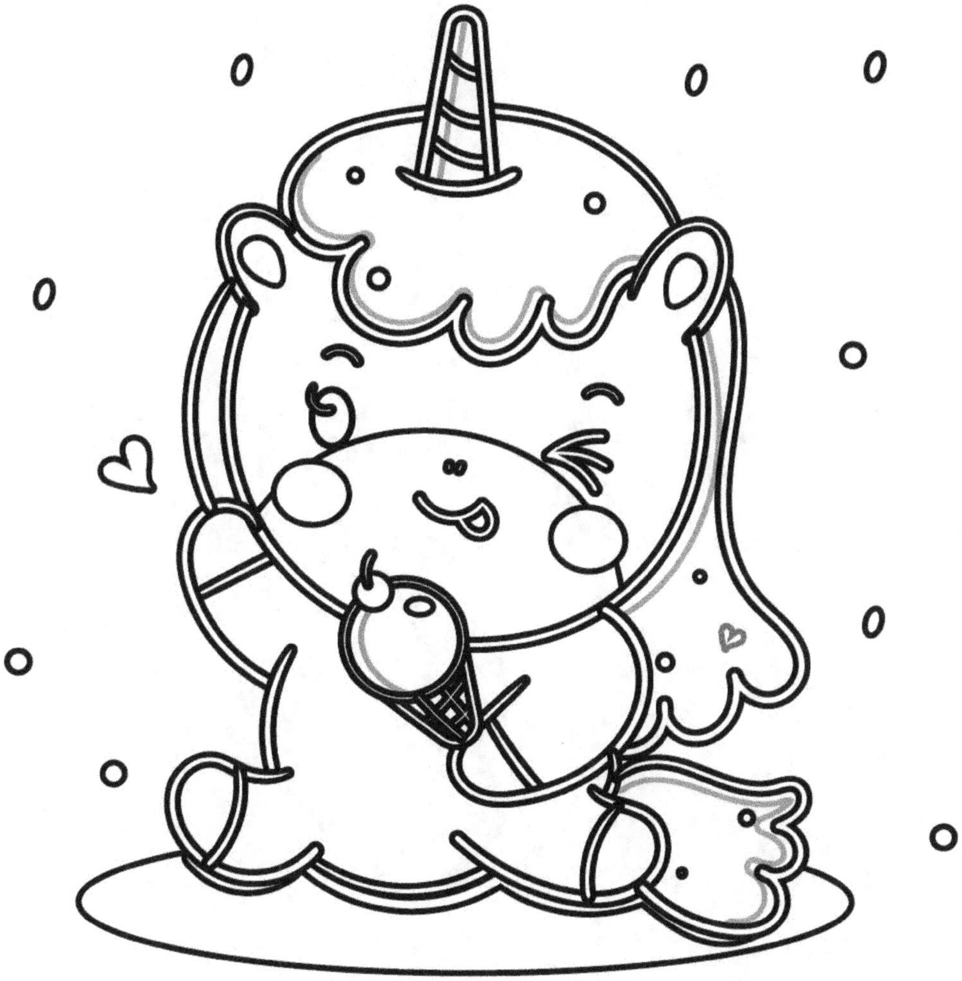

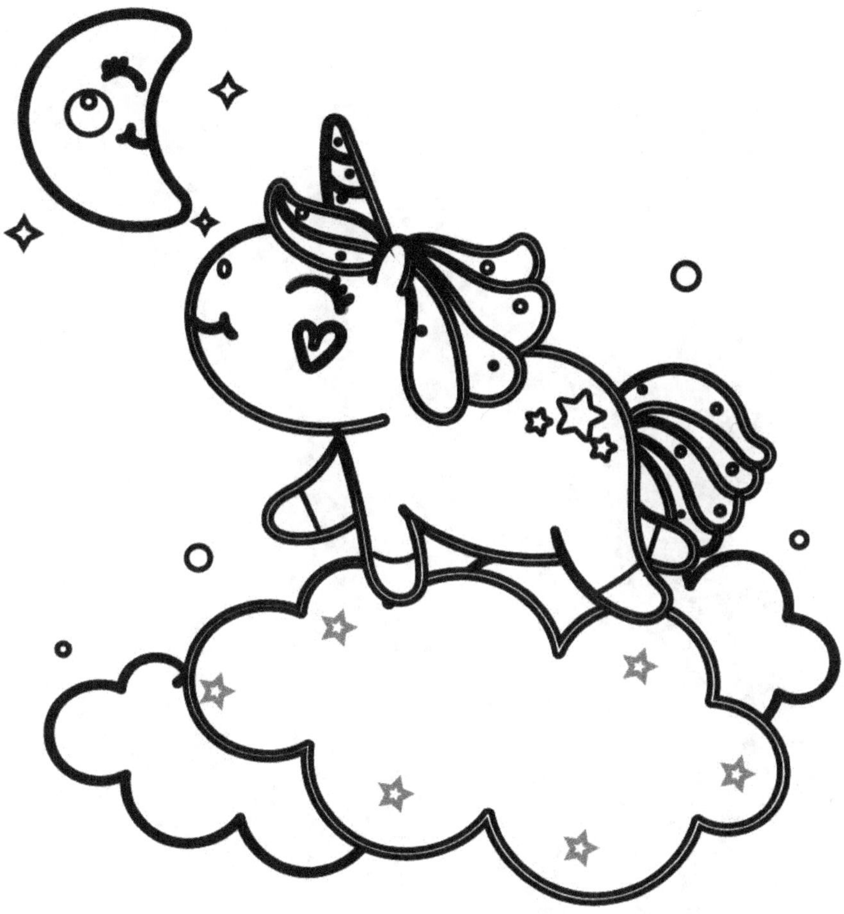

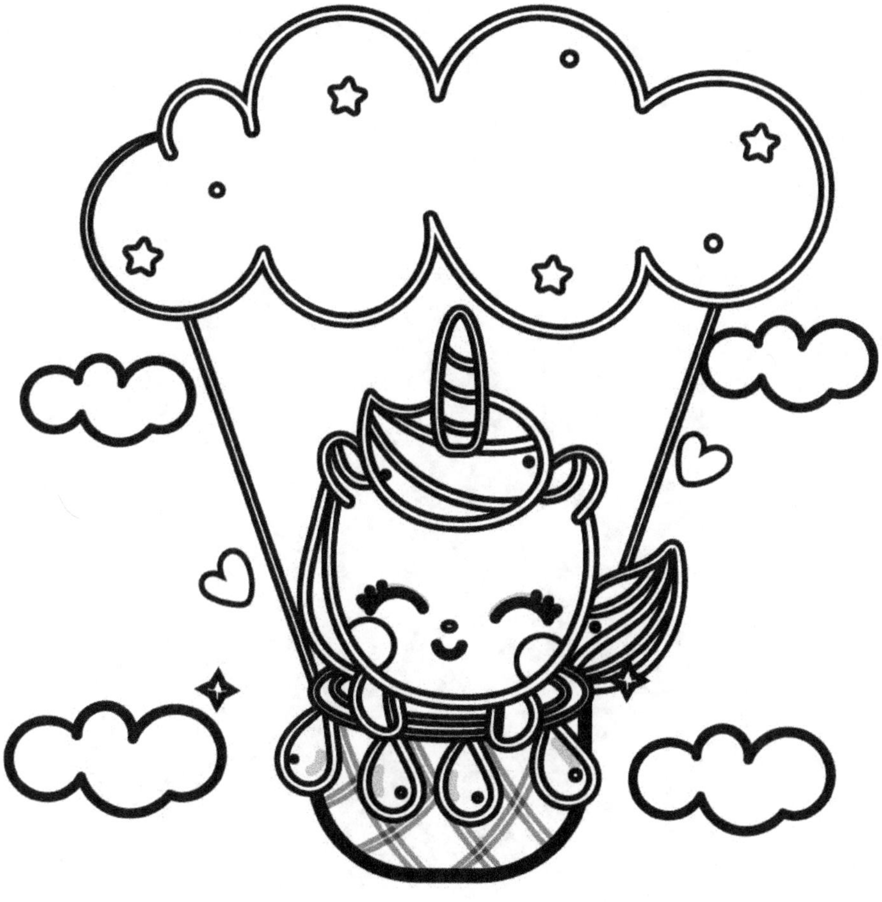

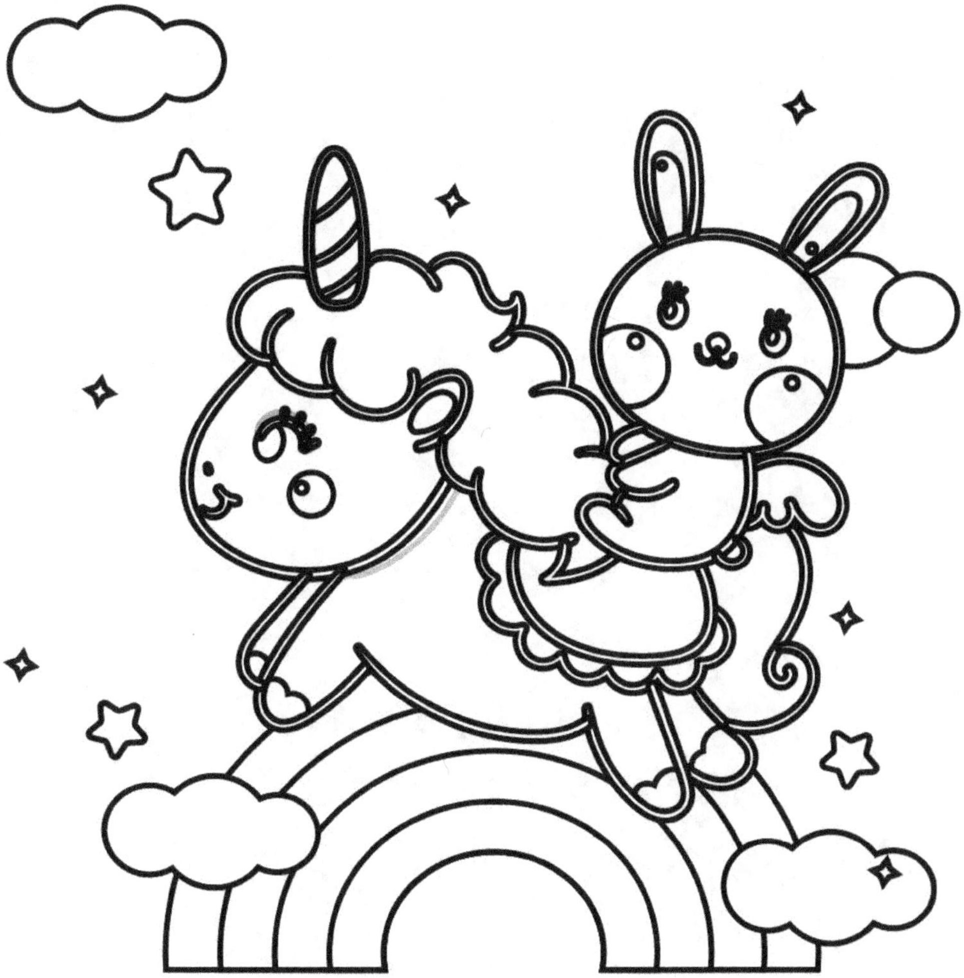

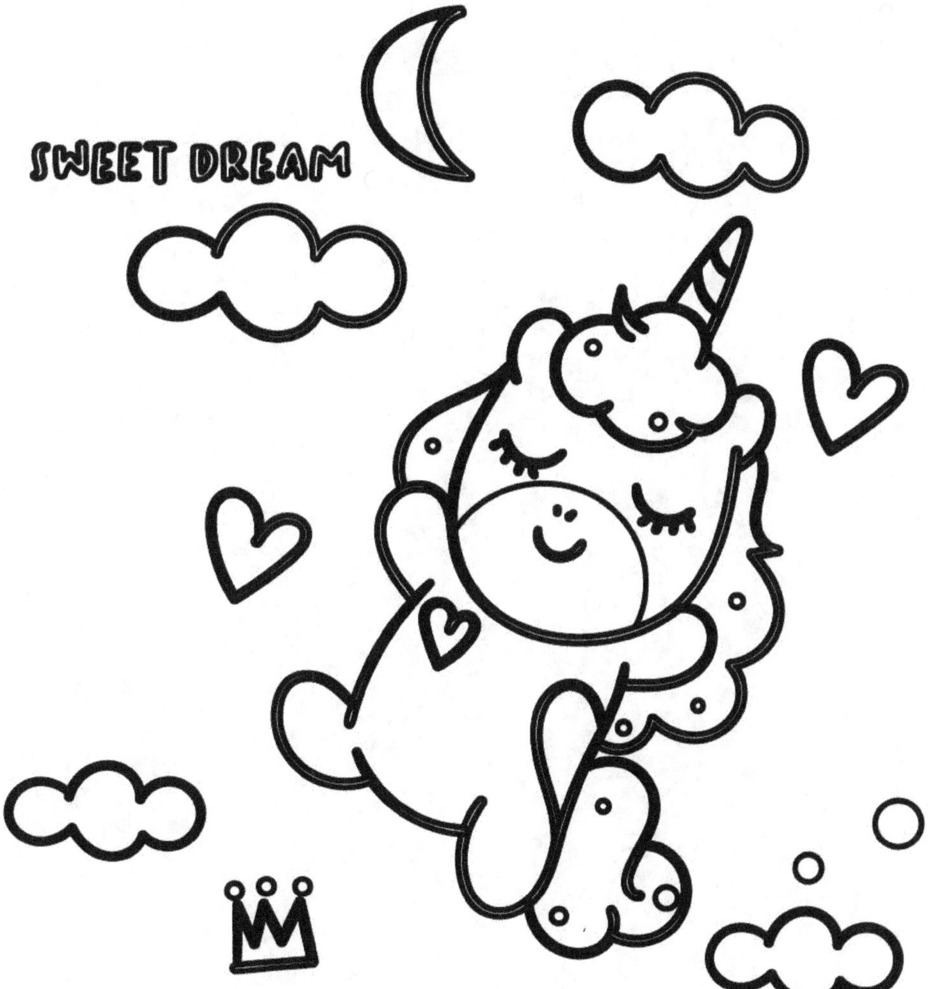
SWEET DREAM

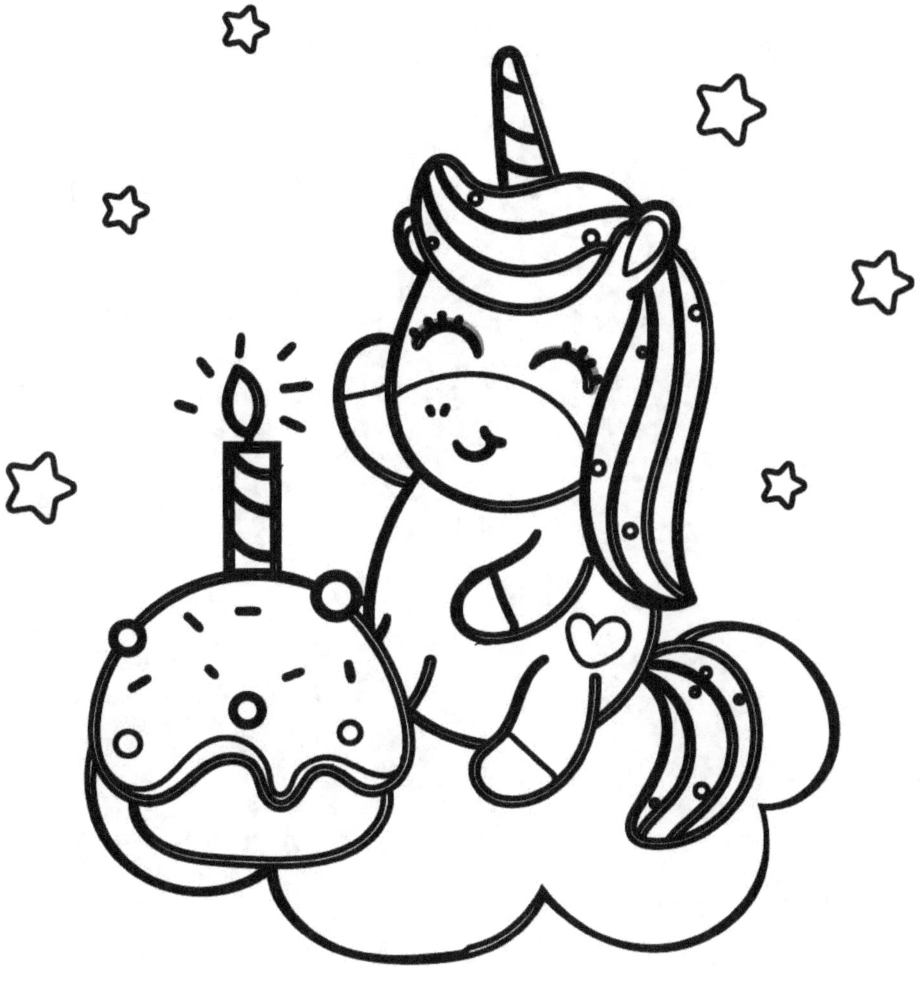

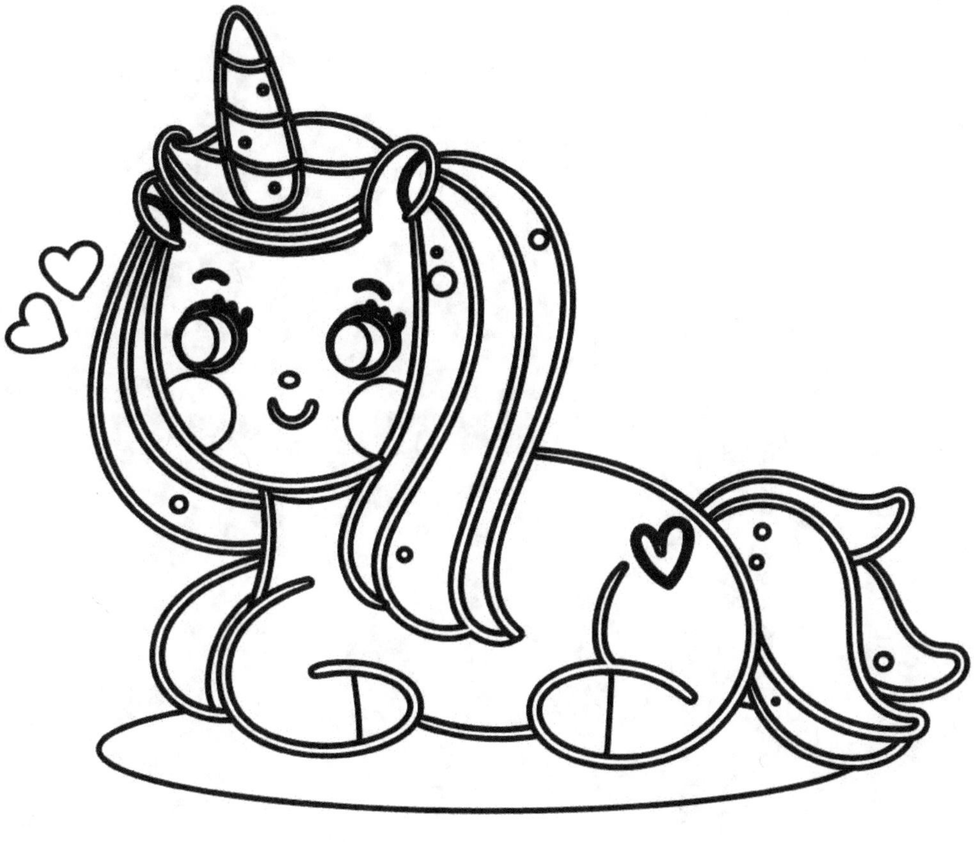

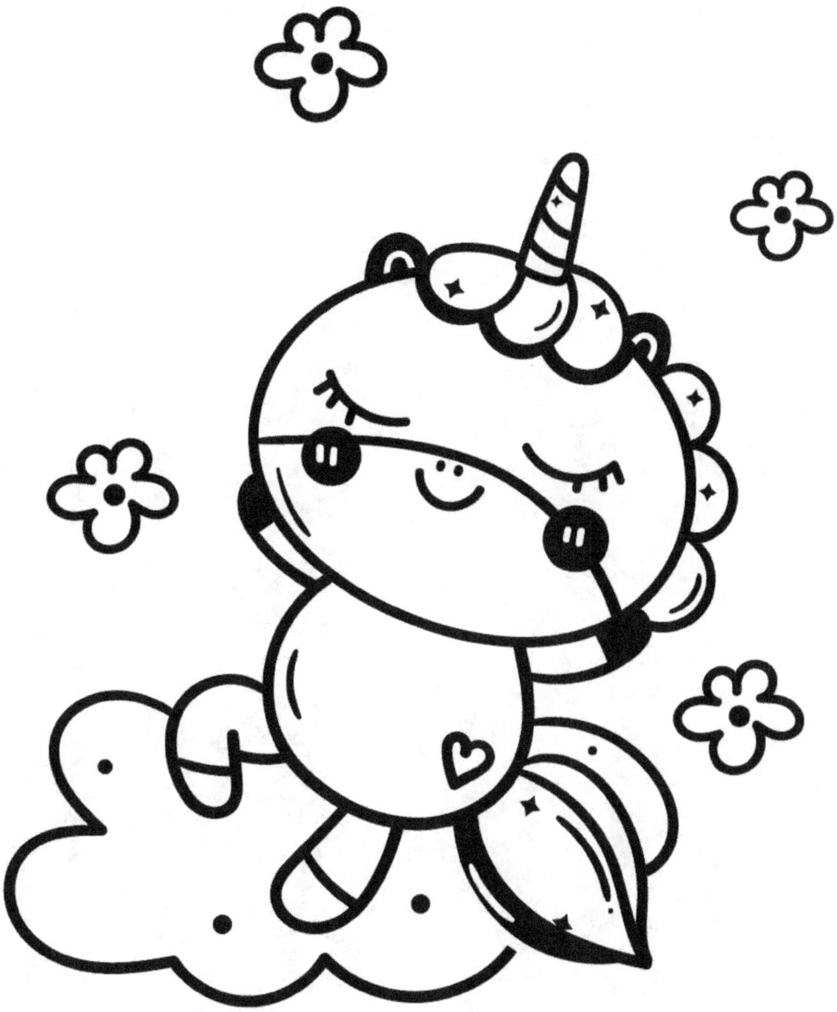

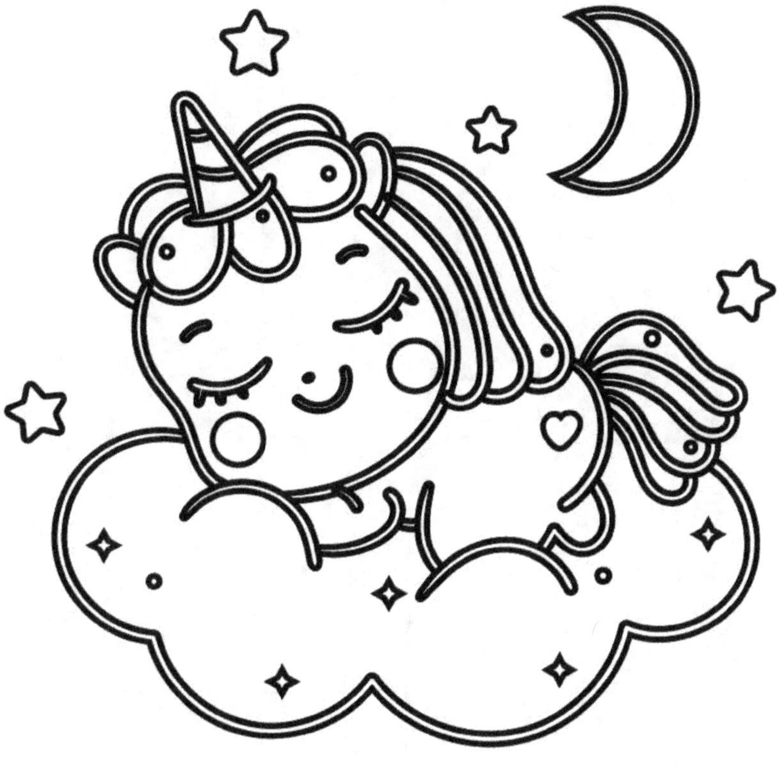

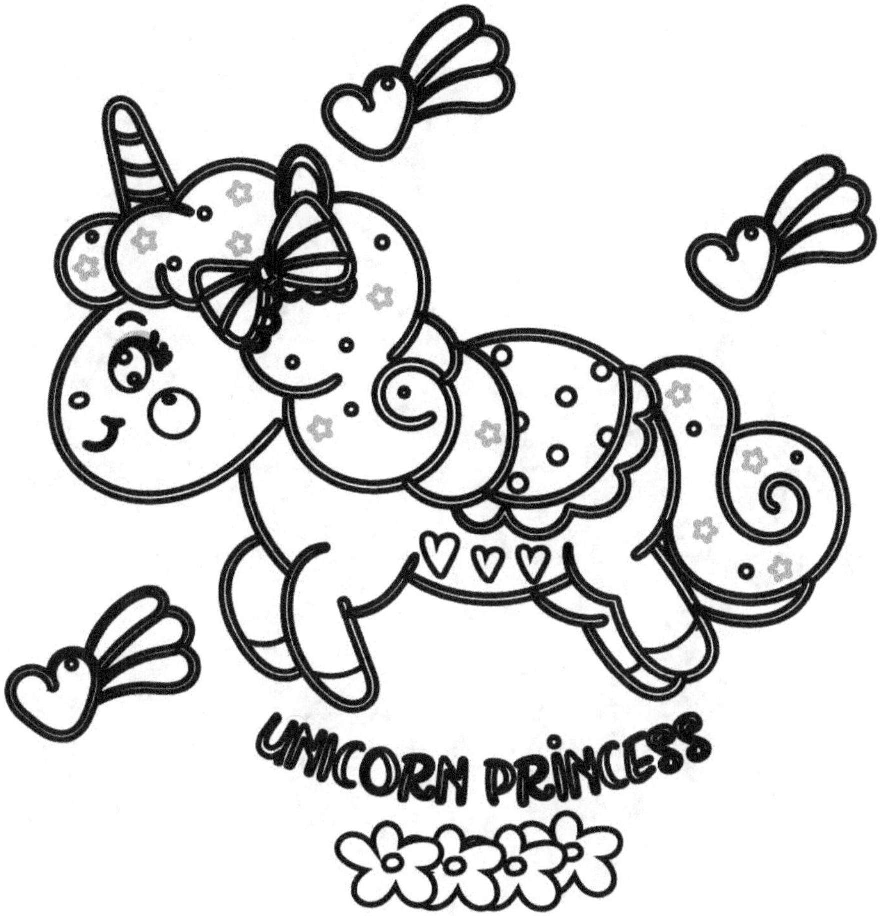
UNICORN PRINCESS

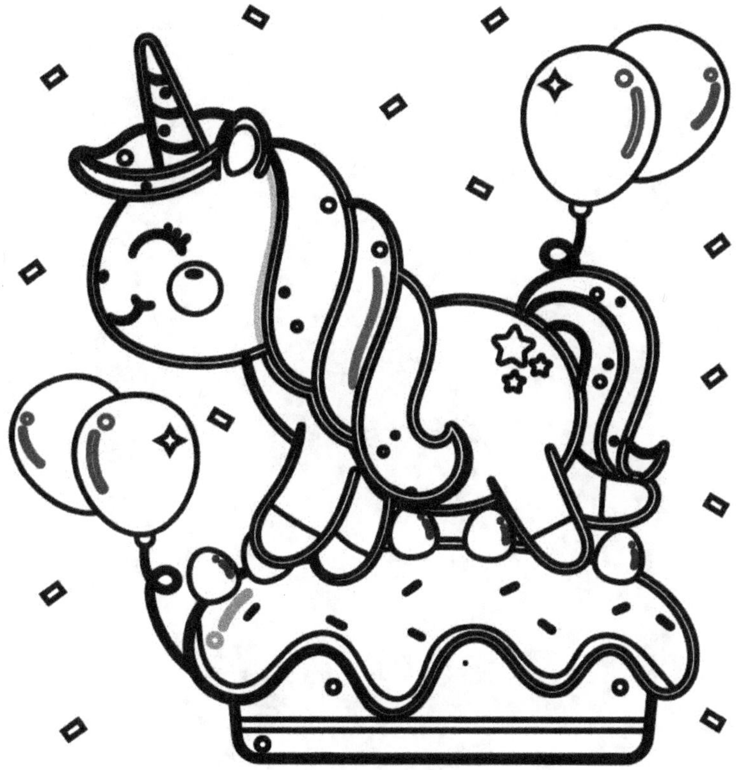

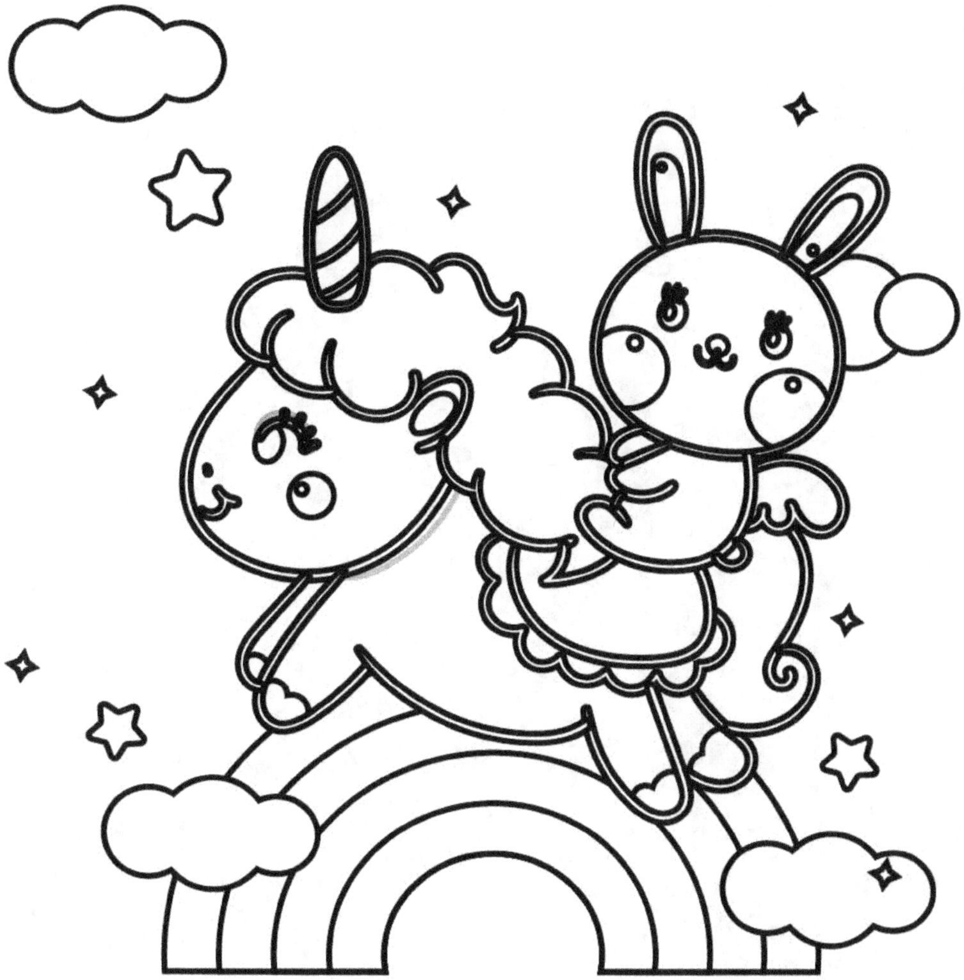

www.ingramcontent.com/pod-product-compliance
Lightning Source LLC
Chambersburg PA
CBHW081604280526
45788CB00011B/3547